Off Leash and Listening

A step-by-step guide to a faster, more reliable recall

KELLY HART

Copyright © 2021 Kelly Hart

All rights reserved.

KELLY HART

Introduction

We've all seen them. You know the ones I'm talking about. The owners at the park who give a single call, whistle, or shout, and their faithful dog bounds dutifully back to their side in an instant, beating their tail merrily from side to side as they gaze up at their human partner adoringly.

Meanwhile, Scamp is a speck in the distance, playing with his canine friends, or chasing after a rabbit, and you're pulling your hair out, wondering where it all went wrong.

Or maybe Scamp comes back – and then proceeds to dance around just out of reach, refusing to let you put the leash on and seeming to never tire of his game.

Maybe Scamp doesn't come back – maybe he prefers to bound up to the prim and proper looking stranger in the distance with their dog on leash, leaving you to go and grab him, red-faced and apologetic.

Perhaps you haven't got that far. Perhaps Scamp has never been off his leash because you're worried about any of the above scenarios happening, or a dozen more you've imagined.

It doesn't matter.

All of that is in the past. Starting today, you and your dog are going to get to work changing your future. And I'm going to be right here to help you do it.

The Thirty-Minute Philosophy

You may be wondering about the thirty-minute philosophy — why train for only thirty minutes a day when you could train for an hour? Or two hours? Or two hours on a Saturday and Sunday, and nothing during the week?

Well, the answer to the latter question is pretty straight forward. Dogs learn best with consistency, and regular sessions help to keep everything fresh in their minds. By training for thirty minutes a day, we make sure we don't undo their progress by giving them five whole days to forget what they've done. Later, once your recall is established, you can train less frequently (and indeed, most of your training will take place by recalling and rewarding your dogs on walks), but while we're teaching them something new, every day is best.

As for why we only train for thirty minutes and not longer, it's important to remember that learning is tiring — for you both. This journey isn't one taken solo. The two of you will be learning this exciting new skill together, and if you work for too long without a break, your brain and your dog's brain will become fatigued, and neither of you will be learning at your fastest rate. Personally, I've found that time to be around ten minutes. Since my goal here is to help improve your dog's recall in the shortest space of time possible, you won't find any exercises in this book which last longer than that.

With that in mind, this book guides you through a series of lessons that are a maximum of thirty minutes of training a day. You'll find each lesson's training plan broken down into exercises with approximate times given to help you schedule them throughout the day. Where possible, try to take at least half an hour between each ten minute block of training, though of course training has to fit in around life and sometimes you'll find you can't do that, which is absolutely fine. Just do the best you can, and I promise you, it'll be better than not training at all. The same applies if you can't fit in an entire thirty minutes of training – just split the lesson over two days.

Sometimes, you may find you and your dog need to repeat a lesson, and that's completely normal. Take your time and progress at your dog's own pace. All dogs are individuals and learn at different speeds. But regardless of how quickly or slowly your dog may learn, by following the guide laid out over the following pages, you should see your dog's recall make good progress in the coming days.

KELLY HART

What You'll Need

You'll need a few things to get the most out of this book:

- A dog (unless you're super into training cats or goats!)
- Toys and treats
- Treat pouch or container
- Collar or harness
- Leash
- A long/training line
- Training cones (or plant pots if you don't have cones)
- A small box or container that your dog cannot open

Getting the Most from This Book

Make Notes

If you're reading a paperback copy of this book, you'll find a page to journal your progress at the end of each chapter. If you're reading the eBook, I highly recommend getting a notepad for this purpose.

It may seem like a waste of time, but try to find a couple of minutes each day to fill it out. It can really help you to pinpoint any problems that may arise in your training, and if you know what your dog is struggling with, or has struggled with in the past, you can really focus on that in your training and fix any weaknesses – which means you'll be nailing your goals in half the time.

Multi-dog Households

If you have more than one dog, I highly recommend training each dog individually so that you can give them your sole focus. This also helps stop your dogs distracting each other. The same goes for any other pets, or anyone not involved in training. Try to schedule your training as some one-to-one time with your dog. Your recall will thank you.

Keep the leash on

While you're working through this book, I highly recommend that your dog isn't allowed off leash on your walks (except where mentioned in the exercises). By letting them run free and potentially ignore you in favour of more exciting things before your training is complete, you risk setting back your progress, and not getting the results you want, and your dog deserves. Try using a long line if they need to stretch their legs, so that they don't have the opportunity to fail.

Location, Location, Location

At the start of each exercise, you'll find a suggested location. These have been designed with security and distraction level in mind. Inside your house is far less distracting than in the middle of a busy park, so you're more likely to have success.

As the exercises progress, we'll build on that foundation of success, training in your slightly-more distracting garden or yard (if you have one), and eventually, out in the most exciting location in your dog's world – the park.

The locations listed are intended as a guide. If you don't feel your dog is ready to be off leash at the park, then trust your judgement and keep him on until you think he's learned enough from the exercises to be able to come back when called. It's better to go slow and steady than to have a failure that sets you back several weeks.

He vs She

Throughout this book for ease of reading (and writing), I'll refer to your dog as he. Please don't take this as any suggestion that you can't train a female dog. With knowledge, kindness, and patience, any dog can be trained, regardless of age, breed, or gender.

Hide the Reward

We'll use lots of rewards throughout this book. It's easy for your dog to become dependant on rewards. Some dogs will then refuse to perform a behaviour, such as coming back to you, until they see the reward in your hand. Luckily, this is something easily avoided. Always keep your reward hidden until you've given your marker word (more on that later) – except where an exercise specifically asks you to show it to your dog.

Not Just What – But How.

Rewarding your dog isn't just about what you give him, but *how* you give it to him. Some dogs will go absolutely crazy just at the sight of their favourite food or toy, and that's great.

Other dogs will still think that the dog in the distance is more exciting than his reward.

When you reward your dog, always praise him with a big smile on your face, and an excited tone in your voice. Throw his ball with enthusiasm, tug with excitement, and make a big production of handing him his treats. Does your dog enjoy sniffing? Try tossing his treats into the grass and letting him find them. Some dogs, particularly scent hounds, will find the searching more rewarding than the food itself, so don't be afraid to build that into your reward system (more on those later).

Low & High Value Rewards
You're going to stumble across these terms quite a lot through this book, so I want to take a moment to clarify them.

A low value reward doesn't mean a cheap one, and a high value reward doesn't mean an expensive one. The terms relate to how much your dog values something. So a piece of cheese might be high value (extremely motivating) to your dog, and a single piece of kibble might be low value (only a little motivating). If something doesn't motivate your dog at all, then it's not a reward, even if it's something really tasty, and you think it should motivate a dog – remember, all dogs are individuals.

Jackpot Reward

Sometimes throughout this book you'll be asked to jackpot reward your dog. This is exactly what it sounds like – your dog has hit the jackpot, and the payout is huge. Instead of just one treat, you're going to give them five or six, and you're going to coo over them the whole time (if that's what they like). Instead of just playing tuggy for five seconds, you're going to play for fifteen, praising them the whole while. Take your dog's favourite reward, and amplify it.

Have Fun

Think of the following exercises as games – opportunities to have fun with your dog. Sometimes, we can get caught up in what we're trying to teach the dog, and forget the fundamental rule of dog training: it's supposed to be fun. If you're not both having a great time, you're doing something wrong.

With that in mind, I want you to make a promise to your dog. If at any stage in the training, even in the middle of an exercise, you feel yourself starting to get frustrated, give your dog a scratch behind the ear and a treat, and walk away from the session. Come back later with a clear head. You'll find yourself much more able to pinpoint what was going wrong, and you'll both learn much more quickly if you're relaxed.

Rewarding Success

In the following pages, you will find an explanation of marker words and reward systems. You may be familiar with both, but I would recommend taking a moment to read through them as a refresher. You'll also find exercise zero, your first step on the path to improving your dog's recall.

Let's get started!

Foundations: Marker Words and Reward Systems

Marker Words

A marker word is a way of telling your dog that he's done A Good Thing and that you're going to reward him for it.

Dogs are sensible – if they get rewarded for a behaviour, they're going to want to repeat it, in the hopes of repeating the reward. But in order to repeat the behaviour, they need to know exactly what it was they did right.

If I ask my dog to sit, and then give her a treat as a reward, she might have performed half a dozen behaviours in the time it takes me to get out a treat and give it to her (sit, look at me, look behind her, have a scratch, etc). She has no way of knowing which of those behaviours is the one that earned her a treat, and it's going to take me much longer to get her to repeat it because of that.

Picture instead, I ask my dog to sit, and she sits. The second her butt hits the floor, I say "yes" – our marker word – and then reach into my pouch. She looks at me, and has her scratch, but because I said 'yes', she knows that the sit is what triggered me to get her reward out. Next time I ask for the sit, I have a much higher chance of her remembering that, and sitting.

You can also use a clicker for this – a handheld box that makes a click when it's pressed. Both work equally well. I'll use 'marker word' or 'marker' throughout this book, but anywhere you see that, you can substitute for a clicker if you prefer.

There are three important things to remember here:
1) It doesn't matter whether you use a clicker or a marker word, or which word you choose to use for your marker, as long as it's the same every time (although single syllable words work best for marker words).
2) Your dog will need to learn what the marker word or clicker means. The easiest way to teach him this is to ask him to perform any behaviour he already knows (eg sit) and as soon as he's done it, use the marker and deliver the reward within a second or two.
3) You must reward your dog every time you use your marker word. The marker is a promise – "You have done A Good Thing, and I will reward you for it."

Don't break your promise, or you'll find your marker becomes less effective.

Reward Systems

That leads us nicely into the topic of reward systems. We'll be making use of rewards throughout this book, so it's important we choose the right one. You won't be using a reward every time your dog does the right thing (although I recommend always praising so your dog understands when they've done it right), but when your dog is learning something new, using good, frequent rewards will speed up the process.

It's easy to fall into the trap of thinking that a simple "good dog" or a scratch behind the ear should be enough, or to assume that a small piece of cheese will be the thing your dog finds most rewarding. With the first option, many dogs just don't find that motivating enough to really drive them (and, to be fair, would you go to work and do your absolute best if instead of paying you at the end of the month, your boss shook your hand and said you'd done a good job? Probably not). With the latter, every dog has his or her favourite reward, and guessing wrong could leave you with a less than fully motivated dog. And for the fastest possible progress and the best possible results, both you and your dog will want to be bringing your A game.

Finding your dog's favourite reward is quite simple. Simply gather half a dozen or more things you think your dog will like, and see which of them gets him most excited. If you have a cup of cheese cubes and feed him one, does he want to go back for another, or is he more interested in the cup of sausage cubes? Or maybe he's looking at his tennis ball, hoping you're going to throw it again. Don't be afraid to think outside the box, either. Be creative.

Reward Tiers

You won't always want to give your dog his very favourite reward. As he gets more confident with a particular behaviour or trick, you'll want to use a slightly less exciting reward. This helps to ensure that your best reward stays special and doesn't become less exciting through overuse.

For one of my dogs, my T1 (best) reward is a tennis ball, her T2 reward is a cube of cocktail sausage, and her T3 reward is praise in an excited voice. For my other dog, his T1 reward is cheese, his T2 reward is pieces of kibble, and his T3 reward is a scratch behind the ear. It's essential the reward fits the dog if you want to get the best results, so it's worth taking a few minutes to work it out.

Possible rewards might include:

- Cheese*
- Sausages*
- Liver paste
- Commercially available treats (be aware: not all are created equal!)
- A game of tug
- A tennis ball
- Beef*
- Chicken*
- Kibble
- Physical fuss

*Cut the food into tiny cubes to avoid your dog putting on weight.

Exercise Zero: Finding a Reward

Choose six to ten things your dog likes, and list them below. Then spend some time with your dog, and number them in the order they most enjoy them.

Reward	1	2	3	4	5	6	7	8	9	10

Lesson One

Day one on the journey to a better recall is the most important. It will be tempting to skip right over this and get to the more 'exciting' stuff later on, but I promise you, you'll have much more fun with all that stuff if you take the time to lay a solid foundation first. It may also be tempting, once you conquer the challenges of day one (which you will), to skip right ahead to days two, three, and beyond, all on the same day. I'm not sitting behind your sofa, or in the backseat of your car, so I won't jump out and yell at you if you do this. But please try to fight the temptation regardless. Dogs are a lot like humans – they learn best in small bursts, with breaks in between. A good night's sleep does an amazing amount to help a dog assimilate their new knowledge, and will set you up to progress far more easily the next exercise, without the inevitable frustration. Ultimately, it's your choice – but if you find yourself with some time and motivation left over, and your dog feels the same way, why not get some extra practice on the day one exercises instead? Your recall will thank you later.

Start by reading lesson one right to the end (don't do the exercises yet), and at the end of it, you'll find the Lesson One

Training Plan – which will tell you which exercises to do and in which order. Lesson one's training plan is pretty straight forward, but they do get more complicated further on, so try to get into the habit of reading the lesson first.

Name Recognition

Right now, you're probably thinking, 'Of course my dog knows his name. I use it all the time.' There's a good chance you're right – your dog very likely does know his name, and it's very likely he's learned to ignore it, too.

If you're anything like the dozens of students I've taught (and yes, I'll admit to being guilty of this one, too!), you use your dog's name multiple times throughout the day when you don't really need or want his attention. 'Hi, Scamp,' you might say, on your way past him into the kitchen. Or perhaps, 'Good boy, Scamp,' as he settles down for a nap. Or even, 'Who's a handsome boy, Scamp?' Because, of course, Scamp *is* a handsome boy, and it's natural you want to admire him. In fact, there's nothing wrong with any of the above scenarios. I talk to my dogs incessantly. The words 'No, it's okay, I was talking to the dog,' are uttered in my house far more than is seemly.

But here's the thing. When we use our dogs' names all the time, they can learn to tune them out, and the name loses its effectiveness. Then, when we're at the park and shout, 'Scamp!' and expect him to come bouncing back, tail a-wagging, we get confused as to why he doesn't. We very quickly forget that ninety percent of the time, when we call our dogs' names, we don't need or want them to do anything. So, when we're at the park, our dogs naturally assume the same rule applies out there. And since you probably don't want anything, the dog is free to carry on with his game.

Are you still with me? Good job on not skipping ahead to day two. Let's get down to fixing this. We want our dogs to understand that if we call their name, we need their attention, and that there will be something in it for them. After all, if we can't get our dogs to give us their attention when they're outside, how can we tell them we need them to come back? The 'something in it for them' is going to vary depending on the situation, but for day one, it will be their T1 reward, or the highest value food item on your list if T1 isn't food.

Exercise One: The Whiplash Game

Duration: Five minutes.

Requirements: T1 treats (or the highest value food item on your list if T1 isn't food).

Location: In the house or garden.

Objective: Your dog will look at you within one or two seconds of having their name called.

Your first exercise is one of my favourite foundation games. The dogs love this one, too, and it really helps to wake their brains up and get them focussed on you. Like all of the games in this book, for maximum effect it's ideal if there aren't any other pets around to distract your dog (or try to grab the food).

Step One

Get your dog to sit or stand in front of you and show them the food. If you need to, give them a piece so they know what you have. You should (hopefully!) now have a dog who is paying attention to you, or at least looking a little interested.

Take a piece from your cup of food, let them see it, and then toss it a foot or so to one side. Encourage them to go and get the food if they don't immediately run for it. No need to use your marker word for this game.

Step Two

As soon as they've eaten the food, call their name. If your dog immediately turns to look at you, throw a piece of food in the opposite direction for them to run and grab. If they don't look at you, move over to them and repeat their name, while holding the food where they can see it, and then throw it.

Step Three

Repeat step two several times, waiting for the dog to look at you before you throw the food. Throw the food in a different spot each time. Most dogs find this game to be huge amounts of fun and should very quickly grasp the concept of turning to look at you to see where the next treat is going to be thrown.

Some dogs will love the running aspect of this game (typically collies, lurchers, shepherds, etc) whilst others will get the most enjoyment from the eating part (labradors, bulldogs, and less athletic breeds). For some dogs, however, the real fun is the finding part (typically scent hound types — beagles, etc). For those breeds, I'd suggest heading out into the garden, and tossing the treats into some long grass so they can have a good sniff around to find it. The more fun your dog has, the faster he will learn. But don't be tempted to work him too hard or for too long – let him play the whiplash game for a few minutes, and then finish.

For best results, keep your sessions short (max five minutes), and play four or five times throughout the day, ideally not less than half an hour apart (time to rest and ruminate is just as important as the training game itself).

Moving On

It can be tempting to jump ahead once you've played the game a couple of times, but rushing will undermine your hard work, and ultimately slow your progress instead of speeding it.

For best results, don't be afraid to repeat a chapter if your dog isn't grasping it. Nothing is quite as frustrating – for both dog and owner – than rushing it and then struggling. Take your time and enjoy your training.

To help you work out whether you're ready to move on, I've included an objective in the description of each exercise. Complete the exercise the number of times laid out in your training plan for the day, and on the last time, count how many times they get it right. If they manage the objective four or five times out of five attempts, move ahead to the next chapter. If they get it right three or less times out of five, then it would most likely benefit them to repeat the chapter tomorrow. If they don't get it right at all, then consider going back and repeating the previous lesson's training plan. Sometimes it's necessary to take a step back before you go forward. Sometimes this happens if you've progressed a little too quickly, and sometimes our dogs just get confused. The important thing is to be honest with yourself, and don't rush.

Lesson One Training Plan

- ☐ Exercise One: The whiplash Game (Five minutes)
- ☐ Exercise One: The whiplash Game (Five minutes)
- ☐ Exercise One: The whiplash Game (Five minutes)
- ☐ Exercise One: The whiplash Game (Five minutes)
- ☐ Exercise One: The whiplash Game (Five minutes)

Total Time: 25 minutes

When your dog is consistently managing today's training plan, you're ready to move onto the next chapter, and the next step in your recall journey, starting tomorrow.

Lesson One Training Plan Journal

Date:

Time:

Which exercises did your dog find easy?

Which exercises did your dog find tricky?

Are you ready to move on to tomorrow's lesson, or will you repeat this one?

Lesson Two

You now have a dog who will look to you when he hears his name (at least, when there are treats around!) From now on, try to call him a few times during the day when you happen to be near him and he's not paying attention to you. If he looks your way, toss him a treat. The more you can build this into your day, the better your results will be once the games get harder. If you have other people living with you, encourage them to do the same – this will help make sure your dog listens to all of the family, not just the one doing the bulk of the training.

For now, it's time to look at your next exercise, which builds on your solid foundation.

Exercise Two: Food Circuit

Duration: Three Minutes.
Requirements: Three cones or markers, T1 treats (or the highest value food item on your list if T1 isn't food), sensible running shoes for you.
Location: In your garden.

Objective: Your dog will run in your direction when his name is called.

This game is a great way of getting your dog excited about recall. It builds on the response to his name you created yesterday, and encourages him to run towards you, having lots of fun. When your dog starts to associate coming to you with having fun, you're well on your way to a good, reliable recall.

Note: You may be tempted to start using your dog's recall cue (here, come, etc) right away, but for now, stick to using his name until we have him motivated enough to succeed. We'll add the cue word in a later exercise.

Step One

Lay out your three cones in a triangle, approximately fifteen feet apart, or closer for a puppy, elderly, or small dog. If you don't have cones, you can use any other visible marker than your dog will be able to clearly see – for instance, a garden cane or a plant pot. A word of caution: you don't want to use anything your dog will see as a toy, or they may lose interest in playing the game with you, in favour of playing a game by themselves!

If you don't have access to a garden, you can use any large, secure space where there are no other dogs or people. Failing that, you can try this game at your park with someone holding your dog on a long line, but put the cones closer together to reduce the chance of your dog being distracted by passersby and other dogs.

Step Two

Put your dog in a stay at the first cone and show him your treats (if your dog doesn't know a stay yet, you can put down a couple of treats to distract him while you run to the next cone, or have a friend or family member hold on to him).

Step Three

Run to the next cone, and call your dog's name in a loud, excited voice. As soon as he starts running towards you, let him see you drop some (two or three) treats by the cone.

Step Four

Run to the next cone before the dog reaches the first one. When you get there, wait for your dog to finish the treats at the first cone, and then call him again, once again letting him see you put the treats down.

Step Five

Repeat step four, bringing you back to the first cone. Continue to run round the circuit following the above instructions for a couple of laps, and then take a well-earned break for both you and your dog! If your dog starts to lose focus or is unfit, then stop sooner. Better only one or two successful laps than half a dozen when your dog isn't engaging with you.

As before, to get the best results from your dog, break your training up into short intervals, and take a break in between to aid learning.

Recall Words

Although for the above exercise we simply used the dog's name (relying on their excitement and desire to get to the food), in the long run you will want a specific word to let your dog know you want them to come to you. We use our dog's names dozens of times during the day, and most of the time we don't want them to come to us, and if they do, we don't reward them for it. While we're training your dog to have a fast, solid recall, it's important they understand exactly when we want them to come, and that they get rewarded each time they do, so they don't lose motivation and undo everything you're working towards.

For this, we need a specific recall word, or cue. You can use almost anything you want for this, although ideally it will be a single word with just one or two syllables, which you don't use for anything else.

Examples include: Come, Close, Here, Side, etc

Lesson Two Training Plan

- ☐ Exercise One: The Whiplash Game (Five minutes)
- ☐ Exercise One: The Whiplash Game (Five minutes)
- ☐ Exercise Two: Food Circuit (Three minutes)
- ☐ Exercise Two: Food Circuit (Three minutes)
- ☐ Exercise Two: Food Circuit (Three minutes)
- ☐ Think of a recall cue word (Five minutes)

Total Time: 24 minutes

When your dog is consistently managing today's training plan, you're ready to move onto the next chapter, and the next step in your recall journey, starting tomorrow.

Lesson Two Training Plan Journal

Date:

Time:

Which exercises did your dog find easy?

Which exercises did your dog find tricky?

Are you ready to move on to tomorrow's lesson, or will you repeat this one?

Lesson Three

By now, your dog not only knows to look at you when he hears his name, he has also come to associate running towards you with having fun and getting tasty rewards. We're ready to take the next step – the part where you manage to catch your dog and put him back on his leash.

Many dogs develop the habit of staying just out of their owner's reach. They're not trying to be naughty, they're simply playing a very fun game with their owner – tag! It's our job to teach Scamp that letting us put his leash back on is in fact far more fun than dancing around the field with his increasingly irate owner chasing after him. No mean feat, but I have faith in you – you can do it! Or maybe your dog hasn't become a dancing Scamp yet, in which case, it's our job to make sure he never discovers this game, because we've already taught him hanging out with us is far more fun.

But to be able to put your dog's leash on, first he'll need to come close enough to you, and hold still. There are a couple of ways of achieving this, and it's a good idea to experiment and find which you (and he!) like the most.

These techniques are great for improving your recall, because they help your dog really understand what you want from him. Often, when we call our dogs to us, what we mean is we want them to come and be near us, or occasionally, when we're on a walk, we want them to come close enough to catch them. This can be really confusing for the dog, because we're changing the goal posts all the time. By teaching him to come to a specific position when we give the recall cue, we can help him understand what we want from him. Suddenly, instead of, 'Scamp, come!' meaning, 'Come and be near me, or maybe come close enough to touch, or maybe just follow me', 'Scamp, come!' now means, 'Come and sit directly in front of me', or 'Come and stand with your nose touching my hand'. And when he understands what we're asking, Scamp can be confident in getting the right behaviour every time, which will really help his motivation for recall.

Exercise Three: The Present

Duration: Five Minutes.
Requirements: T1 reward, and some treats if the T1 reward is not food.
Location: In your home.
Objective: Your dog will sit directly in front of you.

I'll be completely honest, this is my least favourite of all the methods. I include it here because it's the one taught by traditional training schools, and as such, a lot of people will already be familiar with it, and may have a preference for this position. Most dogs don't find it particularly fun, and are wary of being in this position (since we spend a lot of time teaching them to respect our personal space). That said, some dogs absolutely love it, and for that reason, I highly recommend giving it a try. Remember, when we're training, we always want to be guided by our dogs. So, with that in mind, let's get started!

Step One

Put your dog in a stay (or get someone to hold him if he doesn't know stay yet), and take one step back from him. Remember, the objective is the finishing position, not the recall itself right now, so don't be tempted to make it harder for him than it needs to be by increasing the distance.

Step Two

Call your dog to you, showing him the food. As he comes to you, stand with your legs slightly apart and your hips square. Hold the treat in front of his nose and draw it slowly towards your belly button, asking him to sit as he gets close. Once he sits, give him the treat. This position is known as a 'present'.

If your T1 reward is a toy instead of food, you can now also play briefly with the toy (eg, throw a ball once, tug for a few seconds, etc). This will help increase his motivation.

Step Three

Repeat step two several times, until he's coming in close to you and sitting without having the treat held in front of his nose, but making sure you still reward and praise him each time.

Step Four

Repeat the above, but take two or three steps back before calling him, and then reward him when he sits in front of you.

Step Five

Take two or three steps back, and call your dog, then, as he's coming towards you, take another step or two back and encourage him with your voice. Your movement will make the game more fun for him – just be careful not to fall over or it might become a different game entirely!

Exercise Four: The Hand Touch

Duration: Five Minutes.

Requirements: T1 reward.

Location: In your home.

Objective: Your dog will touch his nose to your hand.

By using a hand touch, we teach our dogs to come and stand close to us, with their nose physically touching our hand. This usually starts as more of a bump – a quick touch and then breaking contact – but can be built up to a sustained nose touch if you want. Equally, it's fine to leave it as just the bump if you prefer.

Step One

Ask your dog to sit in front of you and make sure he's paying attention. Hide your hand behind your back, then pull it out and offer it to him, palm forwards, about an inch from his nose. Don't move too quickly or you may spook him. Your dog will be inquisitive about your hand being held behind your back, and will bump his nose against it to check it out.

The moment he makes contact, use your marker word or clicker, and then immediately give him his T1 reward.

Step One A.

Although most dogs will be curious enough to make contact with your hand, some will be a little less interested, and for those dogs, we can help them along a little. If your dog doesn't make contact when you present your hand to him, put a low value treat (kibble or similar) in your hand, hide it behind your back, and present it to him, allowing him to eat the treat. Do this three times, and then on the fourth time, present an empty hand to him. He'll nose it, assuming that there is food there. Be sure to use your marker and give him his T1 reward the moment this happens.

Step Two
Repeat step one three times, marking and rewarding each time. Your dog should now be enthusiastically touching his nose to your hand each time you present it to him.

Step Three
Assuming your dog is reliably touching your hand without any encouragement, you can start to add your cue word. Present your hand, and as you do, say 'touch' (or whatever word you choose). When your dog touches, mark and reward. Repeat this several times.

Step Four
This time, hold your hand a little further away – just a few inches to start with – and ask your dog to touch. You may have to wait a few seconds for your dog to realise what you

want. Be patient, and don't ask him again. Simply keep your hand in position and wait. When he gets it, use your marker word and make a big deal out of rewarding him.

Step Five

You can now start to vary the height and distance you hold your hand at, and be sure to try on both your left and right side. If at any stage your dog starts to struggle, make it easier for him by putting your hand closer to its original position.

Exercise Five: Middle

Duration: Five Minutes.
Requirements: T1 reward, and low value treats (eg kibble).
Location: In your home.
Objective: Your dog will come from behind to stand in between your legs.

Middle is one of my very favourite games to play with my dogs. It encourages them to *want* to be close to you, and aside from recall, it has a ton of uses – for instance, if you need your dog to move out of people's way, or allow a bike to pass, or holding still while you give him eyedrops. It's also a pretty neat trick, and can lead onto other neat tricks, for those who are inclined towards trick dog training. Most importantly, for us, is that it means your dog will come into a position that will easily allow you to attach his leash.

Step One

Have your dog stand in front of you, facing you, while you stand with your legs wide enough apart that your dog will comfortably fit between them (if in doubt, or for a nervous dog, too wide is better than not wide enough). Hold a treat in front of his nose, and use it to lure him round to your right, his left, behind you and in between your legs. As soon as he's there, use your marker word and reward with your T1 reward.

Step Two

Repeat step one three times, until your dog is easily finding the position in between your legs.

Step Three

Repeat step one, but this time, don't have any food in your hand when you lure your dog into position. As soon as he gets into the middle position, mark and give him his T1 reward. Repeat three times, rewarding each time.

Step Four

Once your dog is comfortably being guided into position without food, you can start to add your cue word. Some people use 'middle', I use 'legs', but any cue word is fine as long as it's short, easy to say, and unique to any other cues you use. To introduce the cue, set your dog in front of you, give the cue, then guide your dog into position. As soon as he's in place, mark and reward.

Over time, you'll reduce and eventually get rid of guiding your dog into position, and vary the starting position from behind, in front, and on either side of you. But it's important not to do too much in one go, so we'll be doing this over the course of a few sessions, if this is the method you decide to go with.

Exercise Six: Bonding Time

Training our dogs using positive reinforcement relies on building a bond of mutual respect and trust with our dogs. It helps to strengthen our bond with them, and the stronger our bond, the more likely they are to want to engage with us. No matter how amazing and strong your bond with your dog is, there's always room for it to be stronger.

When we're focusing on something like improving our dog's recall, or training him to walk nicely on the leash, or teaching him new tricks, it's easy to fall into the habit of spending every spare moment with him training – especially if you're new to positive reinforcement, because you'll be seeing the positive changes in the way your dog reacts to being around you, and of course we want to keep building on that, which is perfectly natural.

However, not everything we do with our dogs is about training, and that's one of the reasons I like the thirty minutes approach. It's just as important to spend time with your dog without asking for anything in return. This bonding time will help encourage your dog to spend time with you, including when you're out and about on walks, and other things catch his attention. It will make a big difference to the results you see from this training plan.

Step One
Spend some time with your dog – no cues, no rewards, no training. Just hang out and make a fuss of him. Make him the centre of your attention. Don't be distracted by other people, the TV, or your phone. And that's all there is to it!
Note: Your dog may choose to walk away from you during this time. If he does that, let him go and don't make a big deal

out of it. For some personality types, this sort of bonding can be overwhelming, and it may take your dog time to become used to it. Simply try again tomorrow.

From now on, any time left out of our thirty minutes after training is done will be spent in bonding time – but feel free to do more than the amount I've included each day (so long as your dog is enjoying it: always respect his decision if he chooses to opt out).

Lesson Three Training Plan

- ☐ Exercise One: The Whiplash Game using T3 or T4 treats (Five minutes)
- ☐ Exercise Two: Food Circuit (Three minutes)
- ☐ Exercise Three: The Present (Five minutes)
- ☐ Exercise Four: The Hand Touch (Five minutes)
- ☐ Exercise Five: Middle (Five minutes)
- ☐ Exercise Six: Bonding Time (Seven minutes)

Total Time: 30 minutes

When your dog is consistently managing today's training plan, you're ready to move onto the next chapter, and the next step in your recall journey, starting tomorrow.

Lesson Three Training Plan Journal

Date:

Time:

Which exercises did your dog find easy?

Which exercises did your dog find tricky?

Are you ready to move on to tomorrow's lesson, or will you repeat this one?

Lesson Four

So far, we have taught your dog to look at you when he hears his name, shown him that it is fun (and rewarding) to run towards you, and tested three positions to help him understand what a recall means in clear, consistent terms.

The techniques in the last three lessons will become the foundation for your rock solid, reliable recall. Now it's time to build on those foundations. Today, we're going to teach Scamp your recall word, and start building the leash into the game.

Exercise Seven: The Leash

Duration: Five to Ten Minutes.
Requirements: T1 treats (or the highest value food item on your list if T1 isn't food), low value treats (eg kibble), leash, your dog's collar or harness, a table or worktop.
Location: In your home.
Objective: Your dog will calmly allow you to attach the leash (this may take a few sessions!)

A big part of the recall is being able to put your dog back onto the leash once he comes to you. After all, there's not a whole lot of point in being able to call your dog back to you if you can't catch him when you need to! For many dogs, the leash represents a lot of bad things – not being able to run, not being able to sniff or even walk where they want, and most importantly, the leash being put back on means that the walk is over, and they're going home. Our job is to change your dog's perception of his leash. We start this in the home, so we're not asking him to choose between us and ending his walk.

Step One

Get your leash from its usual spot. If your dog is likely to become over-excited when you go to the cupboard, then get it out earlier and leave it in plain sight. Begin your session once he is calm. If your dog doesn't normally wear his collar in the house, put it on now, and if necessary, give him time to settle.

Pick up your tub of low value treats and call him to you. Reward him once he gets to you, so he is engaged and interested in the food. Ask him to sit, and reward (again, with the low value treats).

Step Two

Pick up the leash. If your dog gets over-excited, put it back on the table, pick up the low value treats, and ask him for a sit again, and reward him once he obeys. Repeat this as many times as necessary so that your dog remains in a sit once you pick up the leash.

Step Three

Calmly clip your leash onto your dog's collar, and immediately give him his T1 treat. As soon as he has taken it, remove the leash. Repeat three times.

The objective here is to show your dog that having his leash put on is a positive thing. We're making him a promise – when I put your leash on, something good will happen, something that makes it worth your while coming and allowing me to do this. However, if you bounce around and do not let me put the leash on, you will not get a reward until you are calm again.

Some dogs will grasp this right away. Others will take a bit more time and patience. Only you know which sort of dog you have. If your dog is the latter, be calm and patient. Remember, time invested in working through this will more than pay you back in the years ahead of having a calm, well-behaved dog who waits politely for you to put his leash on. Be prepared to repeat today's lesson as many times as necessary until you get this essential skill.

Exercise Eight: Naming the Recall

Duration: Five Minutes.
Requirements: Three cones or markers, T1 treats (or the highest value food item on your list if T1 isn't food), sensible running shoes for you.
Location: In the garden.
Objective: Your dog will run towards you when given the recall cue.

In exercise two, you and your dog learned how to do a food circuit. We're now going to put that learning to good use. We're going to use something your dog already knows to teach him something new. It's time to put on your running shoes.

Step One
Set up your three cones their usual distance apart, and leave your dog at the first cone.

Step Two

Go to the second cone, turn, and call your dog – using his name followed immediately by your recall cue (eg "Scamp, come!") Remember, this is a game – keep your voice happy and upbeat.

Step Three

Drop the food on the floor, and run to the next cone while he's eating. When you get there, turn and call him, again using his name followed by his recall cue.

Step Four

Complete three laps of the circuit. If at any stage your dog starts to pre-empt your recall cue or chase you, you're going to need to up your game. Watch him (safely – while falling over will be exciting to your dog, you probably won't enjoy it quite so much!) as you run, and as soon as he lifts his head, call him and give him the recall cue. At the moment, our objective is to make sure that your dog hears the cue, and then runs towards you. It doesn't matter too much if he was already planning on running to you – he's smart enough to make the link.

Step Five

Stop, get your breath back if you need to, and give your dog the chance to do the same. Then, put him in a sit-stay at the first cone, and walk to the second cone. If your T1 is a toy, hide it in your pocket so he does not know you're carrying it. If it's food, make sure you have a good handful of it.

When you reach the second cone, turn and call your dog, and give him the recall cue. When he reaches you, use your marker word, and play with him if his T1 reward is a toy. If it's a treat, give him half a dozen of them, one straight after the other, praising him the whole time. This is called a jackpot reward, and it's a way of helping our dogs understand that what they've done is very right.

If I asked you to take your mug to the kitchen, then immediately gave you £50, next time I asked you to do it I could be fairly sure that you'd want to – this works on much the same principle – by over-paying Scamp for something he's been happily doing, we increase his motivation to do it again. Next time we ask, we're likely to get a faster, more enthusiastic response.

Lesson Four Training Plan

- ☐ Exercise One: The Whiplash Game, using T3 or T4 treats (Five minutes)
- ☐ Exercise Seven: The Leash (Ten minutes)
- ☐ Exercise Two: Food Circuit (Three minutes)
- ☐ Exercise Eight: Naming the Recall (Five minutes)
- ☐ Either exercise three, four, or five (Five minutes)
- ☐ Exercise Six: Bonding time (Two minutes)

Total Time: 30 minutes

When your dog is consistently managing today's training plan, you're ready to move onto the next chapter, and the next step in your recall journey, starting tomorrow.

Lesson Four Training Plan Journal

Date:

Time:

Which exercises did your dog find easy?

Which exercises did your dog find tricky?

Are you ready to move on to tomorrow's lesson, or will you repeat this one?

Lesson Five

You and your dog have both learned a tremendous amount over the last four lessons. Before we start putting all these new skills together and take them to the next level, we're going to work on improving and cementing them, which will be the theme for this lesson.

Specifically, we're going to focus on improving your finishing position of choice. We'll be approaching it from different distances and angles over the coming few lessons, and getting the behaviour as sharp as we possibly can. We want their finishing position to come as naturally to them as breathing, no matter what we throw at them. A behaviour your dog finds easy coupled with a consistent, massive payoff means increased motivation and excitement.

By getting your dog excited about this finishing position, we get them excited about their recall, and we need them to be as excited about it as possible, because when you're at the park, you're going to be competing with other dogs, children… and that questionable smell at the far end of the field. You know the one I mean. If you're going to trump that, you need to bring your A game.

Let's get to work.

Exercise Nine A: Improving the Present

Duration: Ten Minutes.
Requirements: T1 reward, low value treats (eg kibble).
Location: In the garden.
Objective: Your dog will sit directly in front of you from a variety of distances and angles.

Improving the present is about encouraging your dog to come in closer to your legs, come from a variety of different angles and distances, and remain in the position for longer. Of course, we're not going to do this all at once! Throughout the following exercise, you're only going to change one thing at a time. This will give your dog the best possible chance of succeeding.

Step One
Start by revisiting what you've already achieved, so your dog knows the game. Put him in a sit-stay, take two or three steps back, and call him in to you. Once he sits, mark and reward with his T1 reward.

Step Two

Put your dog in a sit-stay in front of you and take seven or eight steps back. Call him into the present, and mark and reward with his T1 reward. Repeat this three times, each time taking an extra step back.

Step Three

Put your dog in a sit-stay, take ten steps back, and three to your right. Call your dog into a present, and reward with your T1 reward. If he doesn't quite find the correct position, use the low value treats to help guide him and get him where he should be. Repeat three times, each time taking one step further to the right.

Step Four

Repeat step three, but this time, step to your left.

Step Five

Put your dog in a sit-stay, and turn ninety degrees to your right so that you're side on to your dog, then take one step back. Use the low value treats to lure him into the present position, and when he gets there, mark and reward with his T1 reward. Repeat three times.

Step Six

Repeat step five, but this time don't use the treats to lure him into position. Guide him with empty hands if you need to, and once he finds the correct position, mark and reward with his T1 reward.

Step Seven

Repeat step five, but this time turn ninety degrees to your left instead of right.

Step Eight

Repeat step six, turning to your left instead of right.

Exercise Nine B: Improving the Hand Touch

Duration: Ten Minutes.
Requirements: T1 reward, low value treats (eg kibble).
Location: In the garden.
Objective: Your dog will touch his nose to your hand from a variety of distances and for an increased duration.

Improving the hand touch is about encouraging your dog to target your hand from greater distances, and to press his nose to your hand for longer. The latter isn't strictly necessary from a recall perspective, and you can still achieve a great recall without it. That said, it does have several practical applications, such as vet visits when you might need your dog to hold still and keep his nose forwards while the vet gives him his vaccinations or examines his ears and eyes, so it's worth your while to give it a go.

Step One
Stand in front of your dog, present your palm to him, and cue him to touch it. When he does, mark and reward with his T1 reward. Repeat three times.

Step Two
Put your dog in a sit-stay, take two steps back, present your hand and cue him to touch it. Mark, and reward with his T1 reward. Repeat three times.

Step Three
Put your dog in a sit-stay, take five steps back, present you hand and cue your dog to touch it. Mark, and reward with his T1 reward. Repeat three times.

Step Four
Repeat step three, but this time take ten steps back. Repeat three times. Ideally, we're looking for your dog to break into a

run, or at least a trot. If he doesn't, try making your voice more upbeat and making the reward even more exciting.

We're now going to work on duration. If you choose not to work on increasing duration, replace the following steps with continuing to increase your distance.

Step Five

Ask your dog to sit in front of you. Present your hand and cue him to touch it. As soon as he touches it and pulls away, immediately cue him to touch it again. When he does, make a big deal of it and jackpot reward him with the T1 reward. Repeat three times. If at any stage he simply keeps his nose on your hand for longer, or breaks contact and immediately re-touches, don't cue him again. Instead, use your marker word, make a massive deal of him and give him his reward. Sometimes, opportunities like that will arise and allow us to shortcut on our training. Always be ready to take advantage of those opportunities as they can save you many hours!

Step Six

Present your hand to your dog and cue him to touch. This time, if he touches his nose to your hand and moves it away immediately, don't say or do anything. Just remain there with your hand in position. Your dog may initially be confused. If he does nothing for five seconds, repeat step five. However, what will most likely happen is your dog will be confused for a second, and then touch his nose to your hand a second time. If this happens, mark and reward him with his T1 reward. Repeat three times.

Step Seven

Repeat step six, but this time you want three touches before you reward your dog. One of several things will happen. He may get confused, in which case, go back to step five, but cue three times, and then come back to this step. He may get confused for a second, and then 'peck' your hand a third time – which is what we're looking for. Or he may touch his nose to your hand, and hold it there for a second. If he does, use your marker word, make a massive deal of him and reward him immediately, don't wait for him to do three touches. Remember, we're building towards that one long touch, and a one or two second touch is a perfect stepping stone towards that.

Eventually, your dog will experiment with doing a single longer touch to your hand. It takes some dogs longer to work this out than others, and it's really important we let him get there at his own pace.

From now on, whenever you see 'Hand Touch' in the training plan, work towards getting that one long touch. If you're getting a second or two, you want to start building that duration by waiting a little longer (we're talking fractions of a second initially) before giving the marker word and rewarding him.

Exercise Nine C: Improving Middle

Duration: Ten Minutes.
Requirements: T1 reward, low value treats (eg kibble).
Location: In the garden.
Objective: Your dog will touch his nose to your hand from a variety of distances and for an increased duration.

Improving your middle is about teaching your dog to get into position from a variety of angles, and over increased distance. This is the only one of the three methods that requires your dog to run past you to find his finishing position. Naturally agile dogs (collies, terriers, etc) tend to love this as they need to spin round your leg to get into position, and will do this at speed. It becomes part of the game for them, and often is as much their motivation as their reward.

Step One

Sit your dog in front of you, stand with your legs shoulder width apart, and cue him to get into the 'middle' position. Reward him with his T1 reward. Repeat three times.

Step One A

If your dog is struggling to find the position, use the low value treats to lure him into position, and then reward him with his T1 reward. Repeat three times, and then return to step one.

Step Two

Put your dog into a sit-stay in front of you and take three large steps back. Give him the middle cue and reward with his T1 reward. Repeat three times.

Step Three

Put your dog into a sit-stay in front of you and take five steps back. Cue him to get into the middle position, and reward with his T1 reward. Repeat three times, each time taking an extra step back.

Step Four

Put your dog into a sit-stay and take three steps back, then turn ninety degrees to your left (his right) so that you're side on to him. Cue your dog to find the middle position, using your low value treats to guide him into position, and then reward with his T1 reward. Repeat three times.

Step Five

Put your dog into a sit-stay and take three steps back, then turn ninety degrees to your right (his left) so that you're side on to him. Cue your dog to find the middle position, using your low value treats to guide him into position, and then reward with his T1 reward. Repeat three times.

Step Six

Put your dog into a sit-stay in front of you and take eight steps back, and one to your left (his right). Cue him into the middle position, and reward with his T1 reward. Repeat three times, each time taking an additional step to your left.

Step Seven

Repeat step six, but instead of stepping to your right, step to your left (your dog's right). This makes it harder, as your dog has to run around your outside leg to get into position. If he struggles, or tries to come around the wrong side, use your low value treats to guide him in a couple of times. Repeat three times.

Lesson Five Training Plan

- ☐ Exercise One: The Whiplash Game, using T4 or T5 treats (Five minutes)
- ☐ Exercise Eight: Naming the Recall (Five minutes)
- ☐ Exercise Nine A: Improving the Present, Nine B: Improving the Hand Touch, or Nine C: Improving Middle (Ten minutes)
- ☐ Exercise Nine A: Improving the Present, Nine B: Improving the Hand Touch, or Nine C: Improving Middle – but not the same one as you completed above (Ten minutes)

Total Time: 30 minutes

When your dog is consistently managing today's training plan, you're ready to move onto the next chapter, and the next step in your recall journey, starting tomorrow.

Lesson Five Training Plan Journal

Date:

Time:

Which exercises did your dog find easy?

Which exercises did your dog find tricky?

Are you ready to move on to tomorrow's lesson, or will you repeat this one?

Lesson Six

We've spent the last few lessons teaching your dog to pay attention when he hears his name, run towards you when he hears his recall cue, get into a position to allow himself to be caught, and to stand calmly while his leash is attached.

Today, you guessed it, we're going to put it all together.

Exercise Ten A: Linking up the Present

Duration: Ten Minutes.
Requirements: T1 reward, low value treats (eg kibble), your dog's collar/harness, leash.
Location: In the garden.
Objective: Your dog will recall to you and allow you to put on his leash.

Step One
Put your dog's collar or harness on, and take him out into the garden. Put him into a sit-stay. If he has a reliable leave it cue, put half a dozen pieces of your low value treats a short distance in front of him and cue him to leave them.

Step Two

Walk ten steps away (don't try to make it easy – use proper sized steps!) and allow your dog to have the treats. If you didn't leave them with him, toss a few at his feet. What you want is for your dog to be focussed on food rather than you.

Step Three

As soon as your dog has finished his treats, call his name. He should lift his head and look at you, and when he does, you're going to call him to you using your recall cue. You've spent a lot of time creating a very positive association with this cue, so as soon as he hears it, he should run straight for you. If not, go back and repeat Exercise Eight, Naming the Recall, and then return to this exercise the following day.

Step Four

As your dog gets close to you, give him the present cue, and use some of your low value treats to guide him into the correct position. Clip the leash on, and use your marker word (it's important to do this after the leash goes on, or he may start to anticipate in future, and that's when you get dogs who fidget rather than letting the leash be attached). Immediately give him his T1 reward. If his T1 reward is something to chase, unclip his leash first so he doesn't hurt himself.

Step Five

Unclip the leash, and repeat steps 1-4, increasing the distance a step or two each time. Repeat three times.

Feel free to get excited and celebrate with him when his recall is fast or his present is motivated. Don't be scared to have fun with your dog while you're training! Remember, if you and your dog aren't enjoying yourselves, you're doing something wrong. Training is about bonding and working together to achieve a goal. It should be one of the highlights of your time together. Smile, laugh, play, and have fun.

Exercise Ten B: Linking up the Hand Touch

Duration: Ten Minutes/
Requirements: T1 reward, low value treats (eg kibble), your dog's collar/harness, leash.
Location: In the garden.
Objective: Your dog will recall to you and allow you to put on his leash.

Step One

Put your dog's collar or harness on, and take him out into the garden. Put him into a sit-stay. If he has a reliable leave it cue, put half a dozen pieces of your low value treats a short distance in front of him and cue him to leave them.

Step Two

Walk ten steps away (don't try to make it easy – use proper sized steps!) and allow your dog to have the treats. If you didn't leave them with him, toss a few at his feet. What you want is for your dog to be focussed on food rather than you.

Step Three

As soon as your dog has finished his treats, call his name. He should lift his head and look at you, and when he does, you're going to call him to you using your recall cue. You've spent a lot of time creating a very positive association with this cue, so as soon as he hears it, he should run straight for you. If not, go back and repeat Exercise Eight, Naming the Recall, and then return to this exercise the following day.

Step Four

As your dog gets close to you, hold your hand out and cue him to touch it. As soon as he does, clip the leash on with your other hand, and use your marker word (it's important to do this after the leash goes on, or he may start to anticipate in future, and that's when you get dogs who fidget rather than letting the leash be attached). Immediately move your hand and give him his T1 reward. If his T1 reward is something to chase, unclip his leash first so he doesn't hurt himself.

Step Five

Unclip the leash, and repeat steps 1-4, increasing the distance a step or two each time. Repeat three times.

Exercise Ten C: Linking up Middle

Duration: Ten Minutes.
Requirements: T1 reward, low value treats (eg kibble), your dog's collar/harness, leash.
Location: In the garden.
Objective: Your dog will recall to you and allow you to put on his leash.

Step One

Put your dog's collar or harness on, and take him out into the garden. Put him into a sit-stay. If he has a reliable leave it cue, put half a dozen pieces of your low value treats a short distance in front of him and cue him to leave them.

Step Two

Walk ten steps away (don't try to make it easy – use proper sized steps!) and allow your dog to have the treats. If you didn't leave them with him, toss a few at his feet. What you want is for your dog to be focussed on food rather than you.

Step Three

As soon as your dog has finished his treats, call him. He should lift his head and look at you, and when he does, you're going to call him to you using your recall cue. You've spent a lot of time creating a very positive association with this cue, so as soon as he hears it, he should run straight for you. If not, go back and repeat Exercise Eight, Naming the Recall, and then return to this exercise the following day.

Step Four

As your dog gets close to you, cue the middle position, and use your low value treats to help guide him into position. As soon as he's between your legs, clip the leash onto his collar, and use your marker word (it's important to do this after the leash goes on, or he may start to anticipate in future, and that's when you get dogs who fidget rather than letting the leash be attached). Immediately give him his T1 reward. If his T1 reward is something to chase, unclip his leash first so he doesn't hurt himself (and take care not to be knocked over while he goes after it!)

Step Five

Unclip the leash, and repeat steps 1-4, increasing the distance a step or two each time. Repeat three times.

OFF LEASH AND LISTENING

Lesson Six Training Plan

- ☐ Exercise Eight: Naming the Recall (Five minutes)
- ☐ Exercise Ten A: Linking up the Present, Exercise Ten B: Linking up the Hand Touch, or Exercise Ten C: Linking up Middle (Ten minutes)
- ☐ Exercise Ten A: Linking up the Present, Exercise Ten B: Linking up the Hand Touch, or Exercise Ten C: Linking up Middle, this time increasing the distance further (Ten minutes)
- ☐ Exercise Six: Bonding Time (Five minutes)

Total Time: 30 minutes

When your dog is consistently managing today's training plan, you're ready to move onto the next chapter, and the next step in your recall journey, starting tomorrow.

KELLY HART

Lesson Six Training Plan Journal

Date:

Time:

Which exercises did your dog find easy?

Which exercises did your dog find tricky?

Are you ready to move on to tomorrow's lesson, or will you repeat this one?

Lesson Seven

If you've been following the training plans, and repeating any lessons your dog has struggled with along that way, you should now have what we call an 'undistracted recall' – or to put it in plain English, your dog will come to you and allow you to attach the leash if there's nothing else going on, distracting him. Unfortunately, out in the real world there are a whole ton of distractions, and you're going to need to be more interesting than any of them.

Fortunately, over the last six lessons, you've spent a lot of time getting credit in the bank with your dog – he now trusts that if you call him, something good is going to happen, and that it will absolutely be worth the effort to come to you. Now we're going to up the ante.

Exercise Eleven: Upping the Ante Part One

Duration: Ten Minutes.
Requirements: T1 reward, low value treats (eg kibble), small container your dog cannot open, collar or harness, long line.
Location: In the house (and later garden).

Objective: Your dog will recall to you in the presence of a distraction.

It's time to step up the distraction level for you dog. We'll be moving back inside the house for this exercise to make it a little easier on him, then stepping up the difficulty as we progress. Baby steps will get us where we're going much faster than risking failure, and they'll get us there with smiles and wagging tails.

Step One

Put some of the low value treats in your small container and set it aside. Put your dog's collar or harness on and attach the long line. Ask your dog to sit, and feed him a treat from the container. Put him in a stay and take two steps back. Put the long line on the floor, and put your foot on it, so that it's not pulling, but so he can't take more than a step further away.

Step Two

Slowly toss/roll the container behind your dog, and immediately call his name – no recall cue, just his name. As soon as he looks at you, use your marker word and deliver his T1 reward (if it's a chase toy, release your foot from the long line). Repeat three times.

Step Two A

If your dog ignores you when you call him and goes for the container instead, use your foot on the long line to prevent him reaching it (so ignoring you doesn't get rewarded), and reset him into the original position. This time, simply drop the container on the floor next to you, call him, and when he looks your way, mark and reward. Repeat three times, then return to step two. Be sure to throw the container gently, rather than hard and fast, as that will be more distracting for him.

Step Three

Set your dog up again as in step one, making sure to feed your dog from the container for sitting. Toss the container, call his name, and this time, as soon as he looks at you, cue his recall and ask him to either present, hand touch, or middle. As soon as he achieves his present, hand touch, or middle, use your marker word and reward with his T1 reward (taking care to remove the leash if his reward is a chase game). Repeat three times.

Step Three A

If your dog comes halfway to you, and then turns and goes back for the container, simply use the long line to prevent him reaching it, and then reset him into his position. Don't panic, this is a normal behaviour, some dogs will get distracted more easily. Simply go back and repeat step two, and then try step three again. Some dogs need a little more reminding than others that humans = payday.

Step Four

Repeat step three, but this time take four steps back before calling your dog. Repeat three times, each time taking an additional step.

Step Five

This exercise isn't called Upping the Ante for nothing! It's time to take this into the garden, where there are far more distractions. Let him have a little sniff around, and then pop the long line on his collar/harness, and set him in a sit-stay, being sure to reward him from the container. Take four steps back, step on the long line (again, please make sure it doesn't put pressure on his collar/harness – the line functions as a seatbelt rather than a steering wheel, it's there for emergency use only!)

Step Six

Toss/roll the container behind your dog, and then call his name – don't use his recall cue, just his name. As soon as he looks at you, use your marker word and toss his T1 reward to him. Repeat three times.

Step Seven

Repeat step six, but this time when he looks at you, give him his recall cue, followed by the cue to present, hand touch, or middle. Immediately mark and reward with his T1 reward.

There's quite a lot of content in there, and some dogs will struggle with progressing at that pace, especially the ones who are a little bit food obsessed. If that happens, don't panic, just take your time and work up to it. When in doubt, make it easier for your dog, and don't progress to the next step until your dog is confidently managing the one before.

Exercise Twelve: Upping the Ante Part Two

Duration: Ten Minutes.
Requirements: T1 reward, low value treats (eg kibble), small container your dog cannot open, collar or harness, leash, long line.
Location: In the garden.
Objective: Your dog will recall to you in the presence of greater distractions.

We're going to up the ante again (hence the cunning name of this exercise!). We're going to ask for the entire recall chain from your dog, and we're going to be doing it in the presence of greater distractions – and without our safety net. As always, if your dog is finding it tricky, slow it down and take smaller steps.

Step One
Fill your dog-proof container with the second highest food reward on your chart. Make sure your dog is wearing his collar/harness, and take him into the garden.

Step Two
Put him into a sit and reward him from the container. Ask him to stay, and take three large (no cheating!) steps back, taking his leash with you. Gently toss/roll the container, and then call his name (name only, no recall cue). As soon as he looks in your direction, use your marker word and throw him his T1 reward. Make this a jackpot reward. Repeat three times, using non-jackpot T1 rewards.

Step Three
Set your dog up again, reward him and leave him in a stay. Take four large steps back, taking his leash with you. Gently

toss/roll the container, and immediately call his name. When he looks at you, give him his recall cue, and once he's coming towards you, ask him to present, hand touch, or middle. Once he's in position, clip his leash on. Use your marker word, and then jackpot reward him with his T1 reward (taking off the leash if it's a chase reward). Repeat three times using non-jackpot rewards.

Step Four

Is your dog more interested in food or toys? If the answer is food, continue to use food in a container for the rest of this exercise. If the answer is toys, switch to a low value toy (something he finds less exciting than his T1 reward). Pop his long line onto his collar, leave him in a sit stay, take three steps back, and step on the end of the long line so he can't fail by going after the container/toy.

Step Five

If you're using a food container, throw it behind him, this time faster than you have been doing before. If you're using a toy, gently toss it. Immediately call him, and when he looks at you, mark and reward with his T1 reward. Repeat three times.

Step Six

Set your dog up as in step four, take five steps back, step on the long line, and throw the container/toy. Call your dog, and cue his recall. As he approaches, ask him to present, hand touch, or middle, and when he does, attach his leash and remove the long line, then mark and reward with his T1 reward.

Step Seven

Set your dog up as in step four – but this time, no long line. (Please note, don't progress onto this step unless you're having absolute success with step six, or you risk setting your training back). Throw the container/toy. Immediately call your dog and cue his recall. As he approaches, cue his present, hand touch, or middle, then attach his leash. Mark, and jackpot reward with his T1 reward.

Lesson Seven Training Plan

- ☐ Exercise One: The Whiplash Game – you can play a shortened version of this, using T4 or T5 treats (Three minutes)
- ☐ Exercise Eight: Naming the Recall (Five minutes)
- ☐ Exercise Eleven: Upping the Ante Part One (Ten minutes)
- ☐ Exercise Twelve: Upping the Ante Part Two (Ten minutes)
- ☐ Exercise Six: Bonding Time (Two minutes)

Total Time: 30 minutes

When your dog is consistently managing today's training plan, you're ready to move onto the next chapter, and the next step in your recall journey, starting tomorrow.

Lesson Seven Training Plan Journal

Date:

Time:

Which exercises did your dog find easy?

Which exercises did your dog find tricky?

Are you ready to move on to tomorrow's lesson, or will you repeat this one?

Lesson Eight

You and your dog are making incredible progress! Yesterday, your dog recalled away from food or a toy that he very much wanted, and stood still while you attached the leash to his collar. That's amazing. You've come a long way together, but you're not done yet.

Having a recall at home is great, and it's certainly handy for when you want to call Scamp in after his last toilet of the night. But what you really want is him to come back to you at the park, and that's our next destination.

Exercise Thirteen: A Walk in the Park

Duration: Ten Minutes.
Requirements: T1 reward, highest value food item on your list if T1 is not food, low value treats (eg kibble), collar/harness, leash, long line.
Location: At the park.
Objective: Your dog will recall to you whilst surrounded by numerous distractions.

For this exercise, you're going to take your dog to a local park. Because we don't want him to fail, we're going to be a bit selective about which park, and when. You want one that isn't packed with hundreds of dogs chasing balls, and screaming kids, and teenagers playing kickaround. Ideally, you want there to be a few dogs around, and no more. The time you choose to go to the park will have a big impact on this, so choose carefully. Remember, small steps make for the fastest progress.

You may encounter a few hiccoughs at the park – for instance, people asking to pet your dog (for some reason, a dog in training is like a magnet to adoring kids!), or other dogs running up to you and wanting to play with your dog, or join in your training session. If that happens, stay very calm, stop training and allow your dog to say hello to the person, or other dog, or football that has strayed into his path. Training can resume once the distraction has gone away again. For now, let's focus on making sure your dog can succeed, rather than putting him at an unfair disadvantage.

Step One

Having carefully selected both your time and location, head to the park with your dog. Make sure your treats are easily accessible. For the first minute of the walk inside the park, you're going to let your dog just sniff and get used to his surroundings. If he happens to look in your direction, give him one of your low value treats (every time!) but don't make a huge deal of it.

Step Two

Find yourself a quiet spot, show your dog his T1 (or high value) treats, and toss one on the floor. Once he's eaten it, call his name, and when he looks at you, toss one the other way. Do this for about ten to fifteen treats.

Step Three

Put your dog in a sit-stay, and take a step back (don't drop the leash, we're not ready for that yet!). Call your dog's name, and ask him to either present, hand touch, or middle, depending on which method you've selected. You may find with the hand touch that he's gone back to a shorter duration, and that's absolutely fine for now. As soon as your dog manages the behaviour, use your marker word and give him his T1 reward. Repeat three times.

Step Four

Let your dog have another sixty second sniff around, and then put him back into a sit-stay. Switch his leash for his long line (keep hold of it) and take three steps back. Call him, and cue his present, hand touch, or middle. As soon as he manages the position, mark and reward with his T1 reward. Repeat three times, each time taking an additional step back.

Step Five

Put your dog into his sit-stay and take ten steps back. Call him and cue his recall. As he's coming towards you, cue his present, hand touch, or middle, and as soon as he's in position, clip his leash on, and then remove the long line (in that order so you don't accidentally let him loose before you're ready!). Immediately use your marker word and jackpot reward him with his T1 reward. If his T1 reward is a chase item, reward him with your highest value food item, then put him back onto his long line for his chase item, praising him the entire time (this is called 'bridging').

Exercise Fourteen: A Run in the Park Part One

Duration: Five Minutes.
Requirements: T1 reward or highest value food item on your list if T1 is not food, collar/harness, long line, cones, sensible running shoes for you, a helper if you have one.

Location: At the park.

Objective: Your dog will engage in chase games with you when other distractions are present.

For this exercise, I want you to be a little more ambitious about the time and location you choose. We want the park to be a little busier, but still not so busy that your dog won't be able to focus. If you do find the distractions are too much, end the session and try again at a slightly quieter time. Ideally, you want a helper to hold your long line, but if you don't have one you can manage without – you might just need to multi-task a little!

Step One

Give your dog a moment to have a sniff around the park and relax before you begin. Set out three cones in a triangle. If you have a helper, pass them the long line and have them hold your dog by his collar in the centre of the triangle. If you don't have a helper, pop your dog into a sit-stay at the first cone and keep hold of the long line.

Step Two

Give your dog one of his T1 or high value treats. Jog a few steps away. Call your dog's name and then wave his treats. Turn and run to the first cone, and have your helper release your dog's collar and just hold his long line (careful not to set the cones too far away or your helper may get dragged, which, in my experience, is a guarantee of not having a helper next time!). When you reach the cone, scatter some treats and call your dog again to keep him from getting distracted.

Step Three

As soon as your dog reaches the cone and sees the food, turn and run to the next cone. When you get there, call your dog and scatter some more treats.

Step Four

Repeat step three until you have completed several laps of the triangle. Your dog should be very focused on you now, and may be running towards you before you call him (which is fine). If not, take a break and then repeat the exercise.

Exercise Fifteen: A Run in the Park Part Two

Duration: Ten Minutes.
Requirements: T1 reward, collar/harness, long line, leash, cones, sensible running shoes for you, a helper if you have one.
Location: At the park.

Objective: Your dog will recall to you when other distractions are present.

For this exercise, we're going to change the rules of the food circuit game and move it a little closer to what your final recall will look like. This might be confusing for your dog to begin with, so be patient, and be prepared to lure him a little more than usual if needed.

Step One

Set up your cones in a triangle, put your dog onto his long line, and ask your helper to hold him at the first cone (if you don't have a helper, put him into a sit-stay). Give him one of his T1 treats, or show him his T1 toy. You can keep them in your hand.

Step Two

Run to the next cone, turn, and call your dog's name, then give him his recall cue. Let him see his treats/toy. Be as excitable as you can while he runs towards you – we want him to be as motivated as possible. As soon as he reaches you, use your marker word and give him his treat or let him play with his toy.

This is a little different as until now the reward has always been on the floor. But now we want him to associate the reward as coming from you. This will help him be more interested in you when you're out on walks together.

Step Three

Once your helper has caught up, have them hold your dog again, then run to the next cone. Call him and give him his recall cue, and mark and reward when he reaches you.

Step Four

Complete two whole laps of the triangle, and then let your dog take a sixty second break.

Step Five

Have your helper hold your dog at the first cone again (or put him in a sit-stay if you don't have a helper) and then run to the first cone. This time, don't let your dog see his reward. When you reach the cone, turn, call him, and give him his recall cue. As he gets closer to you, give his present, hand touch, or middle cue. As soon as he gets into position, use your marker word and reward him with his T1 reward.

Step Six

Complete two laps of the triangle doing this, and give your dog another sixty second break (he may not need it, but the little breaks will help keep his motivation high, so that he's running towards you rather than walking)

Step Seven

Have your helper hold your dog at the first cone again, go to the second cone holding his leash, turn, call his name and give him his recall cue. As he approaches (hopefully at a run!) cue his present, hand touch, or middle. Once he's in position, attach his leash (you can leave his long line on), mark and reward with his T1 reward, removing his leash again if his T1 reward is a chase toy.

Step Eight

Remove his leash (leave the long line on), go to the next cone, and repeat step seven. Continue until you have completed three laps of the triangle, and on your last one, give him a jackpot reward.

Lesson Eight Training Plan

- ☐ Exercise Thirteen: A Walk in the Park (Ten minutes)
- ☐ Exercise Fourteen: A Run in the Park Part One (Five minutes)
- ☐ Exercise Fifteen: A Run in the Park Part Two (Ten minutes)
- ☐ Exercise Six: Bonding Time (Five minutes)

Total Time: 30 minutes

When your dog is consistently managing today's training plan, you're ready to move onto the next chapter, and the next step in your recall journey, starting tomorrow.

Lesson Eight Training Plan Journal

Date:

Time:

Which exercises did your dog find easy?

Which exercises did your dog find tricky?

Are you ready to move on to tomorrow's lesson, or will you repeat this one?

Lesson Nine

You've made incredible progress over the course of the last eight lessons, and you're well on your way to having a dog who not only doesn't run off the moment you take his leash off, but listens and engages with you when you call him, even in the presence of distractions. But we're not quite there yet. Lesson nine is about giving him that final push, and asking him to choose between you and some serious distractions.

Before you progress, I want you to take a moment and review yesterday's progress with an objective eye. Did your dog manage to achieve all the exercises without difficulty or indecision? Or was he struggling a little to focus and stay engaged with you? If it's the latter, spend today repeating lesson eight, and cementing that progress. Your recall will thank you in the long run.

If (and when) it's the former, then let's get stuck in to lesson nine. It's time to grab your running shoes and your helper, and head to the park again.

Exercise Sixteen: No More Cones

Duration: Ten Minutes.

Requirements: T1 reward, high value treats if your T1 is not food, low value treats (eg kibble), small container your dog cannot open, collar or harness, long line, sensible running shoes for you, a helper if you have one.

Location: At the park, in a busy time.

Objective: Your dog will recall to you in the presence of increased distractions.

That's right, I said at a busy time. The busier, the better. We're going to really test your dog's recall today, and that means throwing everything at him. As before, if another dog, child, or stray football intrudes on your training session, stay calm and put your training on hold until they move away. You should find this time that your dog is faster and more willing to re-engage with you as they move away.

Step One

Once your dog is settled, pop him on his long line and pass it to your helper. As before, if you don't have a helper, or they've been scared off by the sheer amount of training you do, you can make do with putting your dog in a sit-stay and holding the long line yourself. Give your dog a couple of low value treats to get him focused on you.

Step Two

Take ten large steps away from him. There are no cones this time, because when he's off leash on your walks, you won't be carrying cones with you, and we want to start getting him ready for that. You can move in a straight line in any direction, don't feel like you need to stick to a triangle.

Turn, call your dog, and as soon as he looks at you, give him his recall cue. As he approaches, cue his present, hand touch, or middle. As soon as he's in position, use your marker word and give him his T1 reward.

Step Three

Repeat step two five times, making sure you reward him enthusiastically each time his gets into position.

Step Four

Put your low value treats into your dog-proof container and give a couple to your dog, letting him see them come from the pot. Walk ten steps away in a straight line, dropping the container halfway.

Step Five

Turn and call your dog's name, showing him his T1 reward. If you have a helper, take a moment to get him really excited before they release him. Give your dog his recall cue. He may look at the container on the way past – if he does, just call his name to get his focus back on you. When he reaches you, immediately use your marker and give him his T1 reward.

Step Six

Re-set your dog's position, take your ten steps, dropping the container on the way. Turn, call your dog and give him his recall cue, letting him see his T1 reward. As he approaches you, cue him to present, hand touch, or middle. As soon as he does, mark and give him his T1 reward and a whole ton of fuss.

Step Seven

Repeat step six five more times. After the first two, hide his T1 reward until he gets into position. By the end, you should find your dog is barely even glancing at the container on the way past, and has long since forgotten about the other dogs at the park.

Lesson Nine Training Plan

- ☐ Exercise Six: Bonding Time (Five minutes)
- ☐ Exercise Fifteen: A Run in the Park Part Two (Ten minutes)
- ☐ Exercise Sixteen: No More Cones (Ten minutes)
- ☐ Exercise Six: Bonding Time. You and your dog have earned some extra cuddles! (Five minutes)

Total Time: 30 minutes

When your dog is consistently managing today's training plan, you're ready to move onto the next chapter, and the next step in your recall journey, starting tomorrow.

Lesson Nine Training Plan Journal

Date:

Time:

Which exercises did your dog find easy?

Which exercises did your dog find tricky?

Are you ready to move on to tomorrow's lesson, or will you repeat this one?

Lesson Ten

Did your dog complete all of lesson nine's training plan happily and confidently? Did he manage to focus on you despite all of the multiple distractions going on around him? Did he come to you every time he was called?

If not, take today to repeat lesson nine. Make sure you're both feeling happy and confident, and remember: getting there is important. The speed at which you do it isn't.

If (and when) your dog has completed lesson nine's training plan without any problems, then congratulations! Take a moment and feel proud of what you've both accomplished together. And then take a deep breath.

Today's the day. The big one. The moment your dog shows you exactly why you've been working so hard from the moment you got this book. Today, he's going off leash.

But only, and I repeat, only, if you have honestly assessed his behaviour over the last few sessions, and are confident that he can recall to you when given his cue. You're the person who knows your dog best. Do you think he's ready? If not, there's no shame in hanging back a couple of days and repeating the earlier exercises.

There's one other factor you're going to need to take into account: how do *you* feel about it? For your dog, there's going to be no difference – he'll be doing the same exercises he's done a ton of times before, and getting the same reward he's so excited about. You, on the other hand, may be feeling a little nervous. You haven't been nervous about the previous exercises, and if you're nervous now, it can make your dog a little unsure. So you need to be honest with yourself: are *you* ready for this?

If you're ready for this, and your dog's ready for this, then it's showtime! Grab your usual pack of goodies and head to the quietest park you know, at a quiet time. I highly recommend a secure park or field, to help with your own nerves.

Exercise Seventeen: A Taste of Freedom Part One

Duration: Ten Minutes.

Requirements: T1 reward, high value treats if T1 reward isn't food, collar or harness, leash, sensible running shoes for you, a helper if you have one, long line if your dog's T1 reward is a chase item.

Location: At a quiet, secure park during a less busy time.

Objective: Your dog will recall to you while off his leash.

Are you ready? Let's do this.

Step One

Ask your dog to sit and give him his high value or T1 treats (our purpose here is to remind him we have the good stuff, so don't skip this bit!) If you have a helper, ask them to take his collar. If you don't, put him in a sit-stay.

Step Two

Unclip his leash and walk five steps away, letting him see his T1 reward in your hand. Take a deep breath. Turn, call his name, and give him his recall cue. As he approaches, cue him to present, hand touch, or middle. Once he gets into position, clip his leash on, use your marker word, and jackpot reward him with his T1 reward (if this is a chase reward, put him onto his long line first) Take another breath. You did it!

Step Three

But you knew we weren't going to stop there. Re-set your dog, either asking him to sit-stay, or getting your helper to hold his collar again. This time, take ten steps. Turn, call your dog, and give his recall cue. As he approaches, cue his present, hand touch, or middle, and when he's in position, clip his leash back onto his collar. Mark and reward with his T1 reward, using a long line if it's a chase reward.

Step Four

Repeat the above step five more times, each time taking an additional two steps away.

Step Five

Re-set your dog, take another deep breath, and put his T1 reward out of sight in your pocket. Leave him in a sit-stay or with your helper holding his collar, and walk ten steps away. Turn, call him, and cue his recall. As he approaches, give him his present, hand touch, or middle cue, and when he gets into position, attach his leash. Mark and reward with his T1 reward, and give yourself a pat on the back, too. You did it! You let your dog off leash, and he recalled to you. Well done, you should be very proud of yourself and of your dog.

Lesson Ten Training Plan

- ☐ Exercise Sixteen: No More Cones (Ten minutes)
- ☐ Exercise Seventeen: A Taste of Freedom Part One (Ten minutes)
- ☐ Exercise Six: Bonding Time. You did amazing today. Take some time to enjoy each other's company (Ten minutes)

Total Time: 30 minutes

When your dog is consistently managing today's training plan, you're ready to move onto the next chapter, and the next step in your recall journey, starting tomorrow.

Lesson Ten Training Plan Journal

Date:

Time:

Which exercises did your dog find easy?

Which exercises did your dog find tricky?

Are you ready to move on to tomorrow's lesson, or will you repeat this one?

Lesson Eleven

Can you believe what you and your dog did yesterday? I'm so proud of you both. You made a massive step on your journey, and although you're not quite done yet, you're getting there.

Today, we're going to celebrate that by taking the pressure off and putting the long line back on. But don't think that means we're going to be taking it easy! Today, we're doubling down on those distractions.

Exercise Eighteen: Upping the Ante Part Three

Duration: Ten Minutes.
Requirements: T1 reward, T3 reward, small container your dog cannot open if T3 is food, collar or harness, leash, long line.
Location: At the park.
Objective: Your dog will recall to you away from strong distractions.

Step One

Put your dog on his long line (keep hold of it!) and ask him to sit in front of you. Let him see his T1 reward in your hand. Cue your dog to stay, and take ten steps away in front of him. Toss his T3 reward (in its container if it's food) behind him.

Step Two

Call your dog and give him his recall cue. As soon as he reaches you, mark and give him his T1 reward.

Step Three

Put your dog back into his sit-stay, take ten steps away, and toss his T3 reward behind him. Call your dog and give him his recall cue. As he approaches, cue his present, hand touch, or middle. Once he gets into position, attach his leash, unclip his long line, then mark and reward with his T1 reward (putting him back onto the long line if his T1 is a chase reward)

Step Four

Repeat step three five more times, making sure you reward your dog enthusiastically each time.

Exercise Nineteen: Doubling Down

Duration: Ten Minutes.

Requirements: T1 reward, small container your dog cannot open if your T1 is food, collar or harness, long line, sensible running shoes for you.

Location: At the park.

Objective: Your dog will recall to you away from extreme distractions.

I wasn't joking about the running shoes part, today's lesson involves sprinting (sorry!) And that thing about doubling down on the distractions? Yeah, we're ready for that.

Step One

Put the long line on your dog and put him in a sit-stay. If your T1 reward is food, put a handful in the container, and then let your dog see you take a piece out, and give it to him – don't be tempted to make this too easy for him!

Step Two

Toss his T1 reward behind him – further is better than closer. Get his focus back on you and put him back into his sit-stay if he's broken his position (don't panic, you've just thrown his favourite thing in the world over his shoulder – it's natural for some dogs to want a better look!) Take five steps in front of him (away from his reward) and turn to face him. Keep hold of his long line so he can't double back for his toy, but make sure there's no pressure on it – you're looking to stop him running the wrong way, not pull him towards you (he won't learn anything that way).

Step Three

Call his name, and give him his recall cue. As soon as he reaches you, use your marker word, and tell him, "Let's go!" Shorten your grip on his long line so you don't get tangled, and run back to his T1 reward with him as fast as you (and he) can. When you get there, open the box and feed him the treats from your hand. If the T1 reward is a toy, grab it and immediately start to play with him. Make this a jackpot reward. What he just did – choosing you over his favourite thing in the world – is a pretty big deal.

Step Four

Repeat the above two more times, making sure you praise and reward him in your most excited manner.

Step Five

Re-set your dog's position, reload your container if needed, and toss the T1 behind him. Leave him in his sit-stay and take ten steps away. Turn, call him, and give him his recall cue. As he approaches, cue him to present, hand touch, or middle. When he does, use your marker word and take him to his T1 reward, using your new, 'Let's go!" cue.

Step Six

Repeat the above three times, each time taking an additional two steps.

Lesson Eleven Training Plan

- ☐ Exercise Sixteen: No More Cones (Ten minutes)
- ☐ Exercise Eighteen: Upping the Ante Part Three (Ten minutes)
- ☐ Exercise Nineteen: Doubling Down (Ten minutes)

Total Time: 30 minutes

When your dog is consistently managing today's training plan, you're ready to move onto the next chapter, and the next step in your recall journey, starting tomorrow.

Lesson Eleven Training Plan Journal

Date:

Time:

Which exercises did your dog find easy?

Which exercises did your dog find tricky?

Are you ready to move on to tomorrow's lesson, or will you repeat this one?

Lesson Twelve

Today, we're going to be building on the hard work you did in lesson ten. As before, if you don't feel ready to attempt this step yet, go back and repeat lesson ten, or even lesson nine if you want to take it steady before moving up to this lesson. There's no rush.

When you're ready, let's get cracking on lesson twelve.

Exercise Twenty: A Taste of Freedom Part Two

Duration: Ten Minutes.
Requirements: T1 reward, high value treats if your T1 is not food, low value treats (eg kibble) inside a small container your dog cannot open, collar or harness, leash, sensible running shoes for you, a helper if you have one.
Location: At a quiet, secure park during a less busy time.
Objective: Your dog will recall to you while off his leash with mild distractions.

It's time to introduce some mild distractions to your recall. After exercise nineteen, this will be a piece of cake.

Step One
Put your dog in a sit, unclip your leash and have your helper hold his collar. Walk ten steps away.

Step Two
Turn and face your dog, and let him see his T1 reward in your hand. Call his name, and when he's looking your way, give him his recall cue. As he approaches, cue him to present, hand touch, or middle. When he does, attach his leash, use your marker word, and reward him with his T1 reward.

Step Three
Set your dog back in his sit-stay, and reward him with a low value treat, making sure he sees you take it from the container. Unclip your leash and have your helper hold his collar. Walk ten steps away, dropping the container halfway.

Step Four
Turn and face your dog, and let him see his T1 reward in your hand. Call his name, and when he's looking your way, give him his recall cue. As he approaches, cue him to present, hand touch, or middle. When he does, attach his leash, use

your marker word, and jackpot reward him with his T1 reward.

Step Five

Repeat the above two steps three more times, each time take an additional two steps. Don't jackpot reward on these times.

Step Six

Repeat steps three and four, but this time, do not let him see his T1 reward until you've used your marker reward. Jackpot reward him with his T1 reward.

Step Seven

Repeat step six five more times, each time taking an additional two steps away (so that your last one is 20 steps away). Only jackpot reward him on the final one.

Lesson Twelve Training Plan

- ☐ Exercise Sixteen: No More Cones – you can play a shortened version of this using T4 or T5 treats (Five minutes)
- ☐ Exercise Nineteen: Doubling Down (Ten minutes)
- ☐ Exercise Twenty: A Taste of Freedom Part Two (Ten minutes)
- ☐ Exercise Six: Bonding Time (Five minutes)

Total Time: 30 minutes

When your dog is consistently managing today's training plan, you're ready to move onto the next chapter, and the next step in your recall journey, starting tomorrow.

Lesson Twelve Training Plan Journal

Date:

Time:

Which exercises did your dog find easy?

Which exercises did your dog find tricky?

Are you ready to move on to tomorrow's lesson, or will you repeat this one?

Lesson Thirteen

Look at you guys go! Your dog is listening to you off leash and choosing to hang out with you rather than pelting off into the distance. Your bond is more solid than ever before, thanks to all that amazing one-to-one bonding you've been doing, and when you're out and about, he's actually looking for ways to engage with you. This is the stuff people dream of – but I've always been a fan of dreaming big. Grab your shoes, we've got some training to do.

Exercise Twenty-One: Tripling Down

Okay, so I might have made that term up. But today we're going to put together everything we've been building towards, and we're going to start putting everything together. Grab your probably-traumatised helper by their scruff, and head for the park (I'm reliably informed that coffee and cake make for great T1 rewards for your helper if you find they're 'busy' when you call them!)

Duration: Ten Minutes.

Requirements: T1 reward, small container your dog cannot open if your T1 is food, collar or harness, long line, sensible running shoes for you.

Location: At a secure park, during a moderately busy time.

Objective: Your dog will recall to you away from extreme distractions whilst off leash.

No waffle today. Let's train. You've got this!

Step One

Put your dog into a sit, have your helper hold his collar, and then remove his leash. If his T1 reward is food, put some in your dog-proof container, and feed him one so he knows they're there.

Step Two

Walk behind him and set the reward calmly on the ground – further away is better than closer. Re-set him into his sit-stay if he gets up to take a look. Take five steps away from him, in the opposite direction to where you put the T1 reward.

Step Three

Take a deep breath. Turn and call your dog's name. As soon as he looks at you, give him his recall cue, and when he approaches, cue him to present, hand touch, or middle. Clip your leash on and use your marker word immediately and tell him, "Let's go!"

Race him to his reward, and give him several pieces if it's food, or have a great game with him if it's a toy.

Step Four

Repeat the above steps three times, and then give your dog a sixty second break to have a sniff around and calm down.

Step Five

Put your dog into his sit-stay, have your helper hold his collar and take the leash off. Toss his T1 reward behind him (if it's food, make sure your container is tightly done up before you throw it or you may find all the dogs in the park joining in your training session!)

Step Six

Re-set your dog into his sit-stay if he moved to get a look, then take ten steps in the opposite direction. Turn, call his name, and give his recall cue when he looks at you. As he approaches, cue his present, hand touch, or middle, and attach his leash. Use your marker word, and race him to his reward.

Step Seven

Repeat the above two steps five times, each time taking an extra step, and remembering to pause your training session if any other dogs come over and distract your dog.

Lesson Thirteen Training Plan

- ☐ Exercise Twenty: A Taste of Freedom Part Two (Ten minutes)
- ☐ Exercise Nineteen: Doubling Down (Ten minutes)
- ☐ Exercise Twenty-One: Tripling Down (Ten minutes)

Total Time: 30 minutes

When your dog is consistently managing today's training plan, you're ready to move onto the next chapter, and the next step in your recall journey, starting tomorrow.

Lesson Thirteen Training Plan Journal

Date:

Time:

Which exercises did your dog find easy?

Which exercises did your dog find tricky?

Are you ready to move on to tomorrow's lesson, or will you repeat this one?

Lesson Fourteen

Are you ready to take the next step? Is your dog? If so, today's the day. You're going to take a short walk with your dog off leash.

Now, when we hit this step, most people have one of two reactions. Either they think, 'We've done it!' and they unclip the leash and proceed to forget everything they've done over the last thirteen lessons – and then their dog gets confused and bored and wanders off. Or they go into panic mode, worrying about every little thing that might distract their dog, and forget to relax and have fun with their dog – and their dog decides to opt out of hanging out with the stressed human.

But you're not going to do either of those, right? (And if you feel it start to come over you, calmly recall your dog, clip his lead on, and have a play and a cuddle.

You can do this!

Exercise Twenty-Two: Checking In

Duration: Ten Minutes.

Requirements: T1 reward, T3 or T4 treats, low value treats (eg kibble), collar or harness, long line, leash, helper if you have one.

Location: At a secure park, during a very quiet time.

Objective: Your dog will enjoy a short off leash walk.

Your helper, as always, isn't essential for this exercise. However, it can be helpful to have an extra pair of eyes to keep an eye out for other dogs, footballs, and alien invasions to set your mind at ease.

Step One

Put your long line onto your dog's collar and take off your leash. If you have a helper, ask them to use a stopwatch to time sixty seconds for you. If you don't have a helper, you can just guestimate the time (don't allow yourself to be distracted checking the time)

Step Two

Tell your dog to "Go sniff", and let him potter around for a few steps. Count to ten, then call his name, and toss him a

T3/T4 treat (if your dog is more interested in running than pottering, just call his name when he gets half a dozen steps away).

Step Three

Continue to walk while he potters (or runs), calling his name every ten seconds or so. You're not aiming for him to come back to you, you just want him to look in your direction. We call this 'checking in'. Continue doing this until your sixty seconds are up.

Step Four

Call your dog's name, give his recall cue, and then cue his present, hand touch, or middle. Switch the long line for the leash, mark, and reward with your dog's T1 reward.

Step Five

Repeat the above steps three more times. If you find your dog is glancing in your direction without being called, toss him a low value treat each time he does (in addition to his T3/T4 treat when you call his name). This is a good thing – it means your dog is starting to learn to check in with you of his own accord, and dogs who check in tend not to wander off.

Step Six

Get your helper to set thirty seconds on the clock. Ask your dog to sit, give him a high value treat, take a breath, and unclip the leash (no long line this time). Tell him to "Go sniff".

Step Seven

Count to five, call his name, and toss him a high value treat. Repeat this for the entire thirty seconds, then call his name, give him his recall cue, and cue his present, hand touch, or middle. Clip the leash on, mark, and jackpot reward him with his T1 reward.

Step Eight

Repeat the above two steps, but this time, set a minute on the clock, and call at ten second intervals.

Lesson Fourteen Training Plan

- ☐ Exercise One: The Whiplash Game, shortened version, at the park with T3 or T4 treats (Two minutes)
- ☐ Exercise Twenty-Two: Checking In (Ten minutes)
- ☐ Exercise Twenty-Two: Checking In, in a moderately busy park (Ten minutes)
- ☐ Exercise Six: Bonding Time. Take some time to celebrate your achievements (Eight minutes)

Total Time: 30 minutes

When your dog is consistently managing today's training plan, you're ready to move onto the next chapter, and the next step in your recall journey, starting tomorrow.

Lesson Fourteen Training Plan Journal

Date:

Time:

Which exercises did your dog find easy?

Which exercises did your dog find tricky?

Are you ready to move on to tomorrow's lesson, or will you repeat this one?

Lesson Fifteen

Wow, what a rush! Yesterday, your dog was off leash with some other dogs in the distance, but he chose to hang out with you instead. Can you believe that? You're doing incredible, and we're almost done here. Let's get cracking with your final lesson.

Exercise Twenty-Three: A Stroll in the Park

Duration: Ten Minutes.
Requirements: T1 reward, T3 or T4 treats, low value treats (eg kibble), collar or harness, leash, helper if you have one.
Location: At a secure park, during a moderately quiet time.
Objective: Your dog will enjoy a short off leash walk.

Once again, your helper isn't essential for this exercise, but may help to set your mind at ease. If you come close to another dog on your walk, call him back in and pop the leash back on, allow him to say hello if the other dog is friendly and the owner agrees, then get his attention back and resume training.

Step One

Ask your dog to sit, feed him a high value treat, and then remove his leash. Invite him to "Go sniff".

Step Two

Start walking round the edge of the park. Call his name every twenty seconds and toss him a T3 or T4 treat. If he looks at you in between, give him a low value treat each time he does. If he starts to drift and pay less attention to you, call him more frequently.

Step Three

After about two minutes, call your dog's name, give him his recall cue, and as he approaches, cue him to present, hand touch, or middle, and reattach his leash. Mark, and reward with his T1 reward.

Step Four

If you need a moment, hang out with your dog on leash and relax. The idea of going off leash is for *both* of you to be able to enjoy your walk. When you're ready, play the whiplash game for thirty seconds, then ask your dog to sit. Unclip his leash, and give him permission to "Go sniff".

Step Five

Walk around the edge of the park, remembering to toss your dog a low value treat each time he 'checks in' with you. Call your dog every thirty seconds (or more frequently if he starts to drift), and toss him a high value treat when he looks in your direction.

Step Six

Continue to do this for about five minutes, and then call his name, and give him his recall cue. As he approaches, cue him to present, hand touch, or middle, and attach his leash. Use your marker word and give him his T1 reward.

Celebrate with him, and give yourself a massive pat on the back. You did it! Your dog was just off leash for five whole minutes when there were other dogs and people around, and then recalled back to you the moment you called him!

Exercise Twenty-Four: Catch and Release

Duration: Three Minutes.
Requirements: T1 reward, collar or harness, leash.
Location: At a secure park, during a moderately quiet time.

OFF LEASH AND LISTENING

Objective: Your dog will learn that going on leash does not mean the end of the walk.

Many people overlook this essential last game. These are the ones we spoke about at the start of the book – the people whose dogs dance just out of reach of being caught. Or worse, take off across the field the moment their owner touches the leash. Now, we've done a lot of work teaching your dog that his leash means he gets a reward, but there's one more thing he has to learn.

Just because he's going back on his leash, doesn't mean its home time. Sometimes it will, sometimes it won't. But if every time he goes on his leash it means his walk is over, it will undermine all your hard work. Fortunately, I have a super simple exercise to stop that from happening.

Step One

Ask your dog to sit, take his leash off, and give him permission to "Go sniff". If you would normally put your leash around your neck or shoulders, or on your beltloop, in your pocket, etc, do that now.

Step Two

Wait a few seconds, then get your leash out. Call his name, give him his recall cue, and as he approaches, cue his present, hand touch, or middle.

Step Three

Clip his leash on, mark and reward with his T1 reward, and then immediately unclip the leash and tell him to "Go sniff". Put your leash away if you normally do this (or intend to in future).

Step Four

Repeat the above two steps three times, always making sure to put your leash away in between letting him off and calling him, even if it's just for a few seconds, and being sure to let him off the second he's had his reward – we want him to view being unleashed again as part of his reward.

Lesson Fifteen Training Plan

- ☐ Exercise Nineteen: Doubling Down, shortened version (Three minutes)
- ☐ Exercise One: The Whiplash Game, shortened version, at the park with T3 or T4 treats (Two minutes)
- ☐ Exercise Twenty-Two: Checking In (Ten minutes)
- ☐ Exercise Twenty-Three: A Stroll in the Park, in a moderately quiet park (Ten minutes)
- ☐ Exercise Twenty-Four: Catch and Release (Three minutes)
- ☐ Exercise Six: Bonding Time. Give your dog a hug. You've both done great (Two minutes)

Total Time: 30 minutes

Lesson Fifteen Training Plan Journal

Date:

Time:

Which exercises did your dog find easy?

Which exercises did your dog find tricky?

Are you ready to move on to tomorrow's lesson, or will you repeat this one?

Moving On

By now, your dog should be capable of going off leash for five minutes at a time without running off, and should come back to you as soon as called, and he should be able to do that with a couple of dogs and people in the distance. And your bond is better than ever.

You can build on those five minutes just by repeating the lesson fifteen training plan and building on lesson twenty-three a little each time. If you did it for a fortnight, and increased your off leash time by a minute every day, by the end of that fortnight, your dog will be off leash for twenty minutes a day – and there's nothing that says you have to stop there!

Decreasing Rewards

Over time, you can decrease how often you reward your dog – no-one expects you to throw treats every thirty seconds for half an hour! That certainly doesn't make for the most relaxing walk in the world.

The trick here is not to just stop the treats suddenly. Phase them out gradually – try alternating your check in rewards by throwing treats for one, and then praising for one, and then back to treats. Take your time with this. Too quickly and your dog will become confused or lose interest, both of which will result in your recall becoming weaker again.

As for the recall itself, please do yourself and your dog a huge favour, and continue to reward every time. It's no hassle to carry a couple of treats or a toy in your pocket, and if you want a reliable recall you need to be a reliable rewarder.

Recall is one of the most important skills your dog will ever learn. It **will** save his life one day. You can afford to spend a few treats on that.

Playtime

You may want your dog to play with other dogs, and, provided both your dog and the other dog are friendly and sociable, there's absolutely nothing wrong with that. In fact, I encourage it. Please note though, I said both friendly *and* sociable. Some dogs are friendly and tolerant of other dogs, but don't particularly enjoy playing, and that's fine. Let your dog make his own choices here, and don't allow him to be pestered into play he doesn't want by other dogs.

If you do decide you want your dog to play, there are a couple of things to bear in mind:

The first is that you're going to need to be more exciting than the other dog if you want to be able to recall your dog away from them. Your bonding and history of handing out excellent rewards should give you a head start on that, so be sure to keep up the good work.

The second is that it's not safe for your dog to play with every dog. Some dogs will be aggressive, some will be scared (don't let your dog be the park bully, even if he just wants to play!), some may be elderly, or recovering from injuries. It's important for your dog to understand he can't run up to every dog, so before you allow your dog to meet another dog, call him in, ask him for his present, hand touch, or middle, and then, when you know the other dog is an appropriate playmate, give your dog the cue, "Go play!"

You can discourage your dog from expecting to be able to play with every dog (and then potentially running up to an unsafe dog and getting hurt) by only letting him play with one in three or one in four dogs. Don't count out every third dog (trust me, your dog will learn to count pretty quick!), just average them out over the course of the walk or a couple of days.

Congratulations!

You've made it to the end of the training plan. I'm proud of you for all the hard work you've put in, and for taking steps to make sure your dog is well-trained, safe, and above all, happy.

All that remains is for me to wish you every success with your dog, and the whole world full of happiness together. Enjoy!

Printed in Great Britain
by Amazon